A HAND TO HOLD

Helping Someone through Grief

Lauraine Snelling

Revell
Grand Rapids, Michigan

© 2004 by Lauraine Snelling

Published by Fleming H. Revell
a division of Baker Book House Company
P.O. Box 6287, Grand Rapids, MI 49516-6287
www.bakerbooks.com

Printed in the United States of America

        Library of Congress Cataloging-in-Publication Data
Snelling, Lauraine.
    A hand to hold : helping someone through grief / Lauraine
    Snelling.
        p.   cm.
    Includes bibliographical references.
    ISBN 0-8007-5950-8 (pbk.)
    1. Consolation. 2. Grief—Religious aspects—Christianity. 3.
    Bereavement—Religious aspects—Christianity. I. Title.
    BV4905.3.S67 2004
    259'.6—dc22   2004000763

To our daughter, Marie,
who lives in her forever home
with Christ himself,
part of that cloud of witnesses
cheering us on.

My thanks to all those who shared their thoughts and experiences, including those I was unable to use. What a wealth of comfort and encouragement you gave.

My thanks also to counselors, pastors, ministers, and all who help these grievers, of whom we are legion.

Contents

Dear Reader

In 1985 a part of my life ended when our twenty-year-old daughter, Marie, died. Her cancer had been beaten once, and we thought God would heal her again. I know he healed her beyond the grave, but like so many of us who have lost loved ones, I wanted things my way. I wanted to share life with her, see her marry and have children, watch her become the lovely woman I thought God intended her to be. She is that woman, but she's in his house, not my world. I still cry, even as I'm writing this, but that's part of life too. It took a long time to get over the feeling of being cheated out of my only daughter. However, now I can give thanks for the extra years we had her with us after her first diagnosis and for the knowledge that Marie is safe in heaven.

I knew I was suffering from writer's block because of my grief, so I'm grateful for a counselor and friends who pushed me and kept pushing me to write Marie a letter, telling her my feelings and struggles. I finally did so. After that I wrote a letter to God; then it seemed the dam broke and I could write again. An article, "Gifts for the Griever," was the first piece I wrote for possible publication; it has been published in magazines, read on radio, and given as a handout by some churches.

One day God pushed me again (he has a habit of doing that), this time to think of using the article as the basis for a possible book. I believe the value of the article to be its simplicity—giving people simple things to do for someone who is grieving. Drawing from my own experience, I saw things that helped and others that didn't. We are not taught how to grieve, and yet grief comes to every one of us at some time. *A Hand to Hold* helps take away the fears that make us uncomfortable around a grieving friend. After reading it, we can remember to touch, to listen, to not be afraid of tears, to push beyond the "I'm fine."

Friends have shared their stories with me through the years, often with valuable suggestions. This book is a compilation of their ideas and mine, all to assist you in helping those who grieve. I gave all of them credit, so when you see an entry without, you'll know that came from me. My prayer is that you will be blessed as you comfort others. God's Word says that you will comfort others with the comfort you yourself have received. He never wastes anything, not even grief.

Blessings always,
Lauraine

Tribute to Marie

Free at last from earthly pain,
You're free to play your favorite game.

I see you there—robed in white,
I see a volley, then a spike!!!!

There is no worry, there is no fret
As you watch that spike go over the net.

There is just pure joy at what you choose,
For it matters not if you win or lose.

Oh, if we down here on our earthly run,
Would learn to do things just for fun!!!!

Elaine Aspelund

The LORD himself goes before you and will be with you; he will never leave you nor forsake you. Do not be afraid; do not be discouraged.

Deuteronomy 31:8

Introduction

Lord, where are you?
You said
You'd never leave me.
But I can't find you
Or hear you.
Isn't that forsaking?
I need you.
With skin on.

"How are you doing, really?" my pastor friend asked. "It's been three years since your daughter died, hasn't it?"

I nodded. It would have been so easy to say, "Oh, I'm fine." But I had promised him that I'd be honest with him when he admitted that he needed help in his ministry to the grieving. So with tears welling, I said, "Getting easier—most of the time."

We had moved out of state, and I was back to visit the church where we'd reared our three children. The congregation had cheered Marie on and had helped pray her to healing the first time the cancer struck when she was fifteen. We enjoyed five fantastic years, praising God for healing her, helping her grow into a beautiful young woman. We even held a five-year anniversary party after the doctors said, "Still clear. You are cancer free."

Three months later the monster was back raging through her system. Five months after that she died. Dealing with Marie's death has been overwhelming at times. As I reflect on the time since she has been gone, I recall some of the most meaningful tokens of caring I've received from others. They are gifts that have helped me through the most agonizing pain I've ever endured. Very simply, these are the gifts my heart still desires.

Touch

Please reach out and touch me. We all need hugs every day, but in my grief, I need them more than ever. If I cling to you, don't be embarrassed. You are God loving me through your hands and arms. Together we can be wrapped in a heavenly hug. And who knows what kind of hope and healing will happen?

Tears

Don't be afraid of my tears, because your fear makes me more afraid of them. I can't always control their arrival, but they aren't the end of the world. Scripture says that in the future "the Sovereign LORD will wipe away the tears from all faces" (Isa. 25:8). For now, let me cry. Cry with me. The tears don't last forever, and we'll both feel better.

Talk

Take time to talk with me. Ask me how I am. Don't let me get by with "fine," because I'm not. Some days are definitely better than others, but the smallest word or thought or scene can bring the memories and the pain crashing back.

However, talking today will make talking tomorrow easier. If I water our conversation with my tears, don't worry. They dry up, and we can even blow our noses and laugh together, because love and laughter lead us on down the road to wholeness.

Time

I've heard that time heals all things, but it is not an easy process. I need you to spend time with me even when I am feeling scared or angry. Don't be shocked or offended if I share frightening thoughts with you. Through your willingness to spend time with me, I will know I am loved. I have no idea how long my grieving could last.

When you want to help me get through this trauma, take some of your time that I know is so precious and talk with me. Touch me and let our tears water a special bond that can grow between us. Like the new shoots of spring, healing can come—for all of us.

Gifts
for Grievers

For I am the LORD,
your God,
who takes hold
of your right hand
and says to you,
Do not fear;
I will help you.

Isaiah 41:13

Touch

Grief is not a contagious disease.

"I could deal with this better if . . ." I stared across the desk at my pastor, those abominable tears brimming again. It had been months since Marie had died, and I thought I should have been over this.

He leaned forward, pulled a tissue from the box, and handed it to me. "If what?"

"If I . . ." I gulped and forced the words out. "If I didn't come to church." I waited, expecting him to frown at me or make some kind of disparaging remark.

Instead he laughed. The kind of laugh dressed in love instead of bleak judgment.

I smiled in spite of the questions wanting to leap out of my mouth.

"Hurts more here?" he asked, his face suddenly serious.

"Yeah, it does."

"People hug you or just touch your arm or shoulder, pat you on the back?"

I nodded again.

"The hymns make you cry?"

Another nod. I forced the tears back down by swallowing hard. This time I succeeded.

"Ah, Lauraine, that's what's good about the family of God. You spend time putting up the walls to protect yourself from more of the grief, and you come here and loving touch breaks those walls right back down. You can't heal with the walls up."

Through the years I've realized that this sense of vulnerability is pretty universal, and it hasn't changed. Being vulnerable is a good thing.

The elderly man was dying, and he knew it. But he had no ties to any church nearby or to any particular Christian denomination. So when the hospital staff asked if he would like to have a local clergy visit, he said, "Yes, send anyone."

I was a young pastor just a few years out of seminary and had put my name on the on-call list at the hospital. When I entered the man's hospital room, it was clear he didn't want to waste time with small talk. So after a brief introduction I asked, "Would you like me to pray?"

"Yes," he answered, as I reached for his hand.

I closed my eyes and prayed silently, *Dear God, please give me the words that this man needs to hear.* Then I waited. Silence. All my words were gone. My easy mental conversations with God, prayers from my Christian tradition, even seminary phrases—all gone. I grasped his hand harder then and stormed the gates of heaven, pleading for the right words to come.

But it was useless. My mind had gone utterly blank. So I remained there beside the man's bed, gripping his hand like both our lives depended upon it. Empty.

At last I gathered up the courage to open my eyes. Tears were streaming down the old man's face. He brought his other hand over to cup my own. "Thank you, Pastor," he said. "That's exactly what I needed."

Betsy Schwarzentraub

I have learned through our grieving experiences that nothing you do for someone who is grieving, even the smallest thing, like a touch on the arm or a simple card, are in vain. My own grieving has made me more compassionate and caring toward others. That, too, has been part of my healing.

Jodi Gilliland

I'd spent several weeks with Mother earlier in the month and returned home when she was doing better. But a few days later I received that dreaded call that said she was failing. I returned to Tehachapi from Texas. I walked over to Mom, gently held her hand, and told her hi. She never opened her eyes, but I could tell she knew I was there by the flicker of her eyelids. She had waited for me to arrive before she would let go. Mom died the next day. As she took her last breath, a magnificent sunset flamed the horizon. My mother loved sunsets, as do I.

Karen Steinlight

I think we always want to "fix" a person's grief. The harder part is to stand by and just be present. After our son died, some of the best gifts people gave me were: a simple hug without words, either in the store or at church; a pat on the back without any intensity; a stroke of the arm as I was talking to someone else. But not only right after he died. For a couple of weeks after. And a couple of months after. I received a card three months after our son died; that was wonderful.

Carolyne Aarsen

Unless the griever lets you know that he or she doesn't like hugs, feel free to initiate them. Those who are grieving often find it difficult to reach out for affection or comfort. Make the first move to give a hug or a squeeze of the hand.

Janelle Schneider

FLOATING IN GOD'S LOVE

I look for God in the quiet places
Of my mind, my heart and soul.
He touches me with His love.
His presence makes me whole.

I close my eyes and drift,
Feeling His warming touch.
I'm cradled in His tender arms.
He loves me so very much.

I float along with Him;
My anxieties I release.
He heals the very heart of me
With compassion and His peace.

Karen Steinlight

I sensed something was wrong that spring two years ago when my father went to his garden spot and rototilled for ten minutes, then came in and sat in his recliner, proclaiming he was "tired."

Days passed, and then weeks. He never went to the garden again, and gardening had been his passion since I could remember. How could this be?

I have since learned that people can grieve without the physical loss of someone dear. They grieve for the person they knew and loved. That's how it has been with my daddy.

We used to take small day trips for Father's Day: the Chinese Gardens in Portland, the Air Museum in Tillamook, train trips, and baseball games. While we were riding, we chatted about things in the past. I couldn't jot things down since I was driving, but I wrote them down later. I'm grateful I did.

My father went from a gentle, kind, loving soul to one who was angry and confused. His anger caused him to lash out at loved ones, not only verbally but also physically. Fearing for Mother's well-being, we had my father examined by several doctors; he was eventually moved to a locked dementia unit.

Physically Dad lives. He dresses and feeds himself and can use the bathroom. But mentally he isn't the father I remember. We've been robbed of that part of him and have only memories to sustain us.

We go—my mother and I—to visit. He cannot hear, nor can he remember what day it is or what he had for breakfast. Conversation is impossible, so I sit on one side and hold his hand, and Mom sits on the other side and holds his other hand, and we comfort him with touch while our hearts grieve for the powerful, strong, athletic man he was, but more for the loss of his once-active mind.

Grief comes in many ways and forms. I lean on God and pray for courage and strength for what I know will come.

Birdie Etchison

Those who sow in tears will reap with songs of joy.

Psalm 126:5

Tears

*There is great healing
in the shedding of many tears.*

Fr. Richard Williams

"Will you still be able to come?"

I listened to the voice on the phone, shaking my head, as my soul shook within. *I cannot do this.* Nearly a year earlier I had agreed to lead a church women's retreat in Idaho. I now lived in California, and Marie had died three weeks earlier.

Somehow the woman calling me had learned of our loss.

"We will understand if you feel you can't come." Her voice conveyed sympathy, empathy. By this time the two words were indistinguishable in meaning to me.

I mopped the tears that her kindness incited and sighed. *Of course I cannot do this.*

Why not?

Sometimes I wanted to scream at that voice in my soul. I only screamed at God. *You knew this was going to happen, and you could have prevented it. You did nothing; you let her die.* The thoughts whipped through my mind, thoughts that attacked without provocation, let alone this reminder that I had agreed to lead a retreat—on forgiveness. Oh, the irony of it all. I had worked on my presentations, dividing the topic in three: Forgiving others, forgiving oneself, forgiving God.

Yes, I knew, and I will get you through this.

I slumped in a nearby chair, phone clamped between shoulder and ear. *You mean you want me to go?*

My caller described the Sawtooth Mountains, the lakes, and the trees that surrounded the Bible camp. "Perhaps the beauty of this place will help you."

I will be with you.

That part I knew. No matter how I railed against him, I knew with all the certainty of my grief-riddled soul that God had not deserted me. I knew that Marie was safe within his arms and was experiencing the joys of heaven.

I sucked in a deep breath, bit my lower lip until it ached, and nodded. "I'll come."

"If you're sure . . ."

"I'm sure."

She gave me the instructions as to my trip and said my flight information and tickets would be in the mail.

Somehow I did everything that had to be done in preparation, made the trip, and led the retreat. Until the session on forgiving God.

Everyone in attendance knew my story by now, and when I admitted that at this point I still could not forgive God, I stood with more tears pouring from my heart and leaking down my face. Others admitted they couldn't either. Some confessed their lack of forgiveness for a friend or family member. We all prayed that God would show us how to forgive because he first forgave us.

During the break a dear woman came up to me with a Bible verse written on a piece of paper. Hugging me, she said, "He loves you, you know; in fact, far more than you know. He loves you so much he has stored all your tears in a bottle. It says so in Psalms."

I looked at the verse written on the paper.

> You have kept count of my tossings;
>   put my tears in your bottle.
> Are they not in your record?
>
> Psalm 56:8 NRSV

"I don't remember ever reading that," I confessed.

"The Bible is like that." She hugged me again.

All my tears in a bottle. All the oceans of tears I have cried since Marie got sick. In a bottle.

Thank you, my God, my Father.

THOSE WHO GO BEFORE US

When they left us,
As they went to the other side,
Our tears fell like rain,
Our grief we could not hide.

But we who believe in Christ
Know our loved ones are with Him.
Their souls have flown to heaven.
Our future's not so grim.

Yes, we believers grieve,
But not without hope.
Someday we'll join our loved ones.
For now, in this life, we must cope.

We will continue on this earth,
For we still have a job to do;
We'll join our heavenly family
When our work down here is through.

So hold your chin up high
Though tears roll down your face;
We know that those who've left before us
Are in a far better place!

Karen Steinlight

This quote from Virginia Barckley is one that for over twenty years has profoundly colored my view of life and death. I found it in some material used by the hospice training program in Ellsworth, Kansas.

> All grief must not be thought of as dreary and destructive. The world would be worse without it. If no man's life were significant enough to cause weeping, if birth and death were unmarked, if the measure of our years on earth were nothing, we might better be houseflies rather than human beings, made in God's image. Profound grief is preceded by deep love which gives life meaning. In the deepest sense, our days would be empty and futile if we never grieved, or never, dying, left emotional chaos behind us.

The idea that grieving indicates that we have enjoyed a relationship of deep love and respect is very comforting to me. And it causes me to want to live my life in such a way that I leave behind as much "emotional chaos" as possible when I go.

Deborah Raney

I said, "God, I hurt."
And God said, "I know."

I said, "God, I cry a lot."
And God said, "That is why I gave you tears."

I said, "God, I am so depressed."
And God said, " That is why I gave you sun-
    shine."

I said, "God, life is so hard."
And God said, "That is why I gave you loved
    ones."

I said, "God, my loved one died."
And God said, "So did mine."

I said, "God, but it is such a loss."
And God said, "I saw mine nailed to a cross."

I said, "God, but your loved one lives."
And God said, "Mine is on my right and
yours is in the light."

I said, "God, it hurts."
And God said, "I know."

author unknown
(placed at Oklahoma City bombing site)

*There is a time
      for everything,
and a season
      for every activity
      under heaven: . . .
a time to be silent
      and a time to speak.*

Ecclesiastes 3:1, 27

Talk

This is part of the task of friends — to help keep the memory of the loved one alive.

Granger E. Westberg in *Good Grief*

"If I've described what happened once, I'm sure I've told it a hundred times until I'm sick of it." I looked at my journal entry and nodded. Not only have I told it those many times, I've written it more than once also. Will this need never go away? I've wanted to crawl in a hole and pull the opening in after me so I can't talk to anyone, but that doesn't seem to be an option. At least not for me.

And yet they, those who know far more about grief and grieving than I do, tell me this is a normal part of the grieving process. That it is far healthier to talk it out than to stuff it.

Looking back, I can see that the experts are right. The urge to tell the story of Marie's death and all the events after that finally disappeared, as have many of

the memories, especially the bad ones. I am thankful
that God answers prayers, for I prayed that these bad
memories would be gone. Now I can tell new grievers
that this need to talk so much too shall pass. I am grateful all these years later for the friends who took the time
to listen to me and be part of my healing.

Recently, my husband, Jack, who is a pastor, officiated at the funeral of an elderly man who had been married for sixty-two years. The couple loved Jesus and loved each other deeply. Jack and I stood at the casket and watched the widow throw herself over the open casket, sobbing with grief.

When she stood up, the family asked me to care for her while they finished up details before leaving for the cemetery. I felt panic. I thought, *What do I do? What do I say? How do I respond to grief I can't begin to imagine?* I was crying just watching her; a lot of good I was. *I don't want to be up close and personal to such raw grief. She doesn't know me that well. Surely someone else should be with her at such a personal, private moment.*

I put my arm around her and helped her to a nearby couch, then held her hand as she composed herself. It didn't take long before she initiated small talk. I agreed with her that the service was wonderful and the flowers were beautiful and her granddaughter gave a lovely eulogy. It was then I realized I was the best one for the job; the family needed to be elsewhere, but Irene needed someone with her. I had also done the best thing—to just be there. I needed to be still, to be available, and to listen when needed.

Karen Wingate

The best gift I think you can give? Let the grieving people talk about their loved one. Ignore the tears; hand them a tissue and let them wipe their eyes and talk. Don't be afraid to shed your own tears, but don't get caught up in your sorrow. Share your own stories about their loved one, especially the funny ones. Let the griever know that their memories—all they have left—are important to you too. Talk about the person as if you were talking about someone still alive, but not around at the moment. This might happen more easily a month or two after the loved one has died.

Carolyne Aarsen

Grieving actually begins before death, because people know they're dying. We need to be there with them to talk and pray—to be as natural as we can, to keep them in the land of the living, not shut them away into a dimly lit area where they feel they're already half dead. We should sing together, make jokes, talk about heaven, talk about our past joys and sorrows, keep them part of the family and circle of friends.

When my friend was dying, her mother told everyone to stay away, so her other friends and I did as told. We stayed away. But I began to feel guilty, so I went one day to visit my friend. She looked up with huge eyes in a sunken face with tubes protruding from her nose and said, "Where have you been? I missed you." My friend later died at home with her family around her, even her little daughter, Sonja (whom I babysat), and they sang songs as she walked into glory.

I remember sitting with a young boy who was dying, telling him stories, patting him, praying.

I also spent time with another dying friend, talking with her, telling her office gossip, praying, laughing. Later, when she lay immobile on the bed in a fetal position, I smoothed her arms, prayed with her, and talked to her.

When my aunt was dying of lung cancer, I prayed with her, leaning close to her ear.

I regret that I didn't talk to my mother when she was dying; she was in a coma, and I thought she couldn't hear. It broke my heart when I found out she could have heard me; it's a deep sorrow for me. I prayed with her and patted her, but I should have stayed longer to just talk.

I hope if I'm ever in a slow dying state that people will come to visit, to laugh and joke and talk and be natural. I do pray for this.

Gail Denham

When I was about twenty-four, incredibly young and naive, my uncle's mother died. I'd never had much contact with her, but when I was much younger, she'd knitted me some slippers and crochet-covered some coat hangers. I told my uncle that I had outgrown the slippers but still had the coat hangers in my closet, and I would never forget her because of them.

He later said that my note had deeply touched him.

I realized that grievers want to hear a personal remembrance of their deceased loved one. Too often we tippy-toe around mourners, as if not mentioning their loss will help them forget. Grievers don't want to forget; they want to remember. It's what they cling to, especially in the darkest of days. Shared memories are like bits of colored glass in a stained glass window. Each piece, no matter how small, can fit into a beautiful mosaic for the griever to study, smile at, and cry over. Is there anything more brilliant than sun shining through a stained glass window? So it is with memories of the deceased, when we share them with their grievers.

Jane Orcutt

No matter what the griever says, assure him or her that what he or she feels is normal. Often the griever is sure that his or her feelings are too strong to be normal, or too strange, or whatever. Numbness, anger, depression—they're all part of the package. The anger phase seems most difficult for Christians to handle, particularly since they often feel angry at God for allowing their loved one to die. Assure the griever that anger is normal, that God can handle that person's anger, and that "this, too, shall pass."

Be careful about citing personal experiences or saying, "I know how you feel." Even if your loss seems remarkably similar to what the griever is experiencing, there are layers of emotion and memory you can't possibly know. Remember that this grief is about the griever; keep your focus on him or her. Feel free to say, "I don't know what to say, but I'm here for you." The person who is grieving doesn't want to be "fixed" but rather, heard and loved.

Janelle Schneider

The phone rang as we came through the door on our return from a vacation trip. My husband answered and reacted strongly to something said to him. I tried to listen too, but he turned his back and motioned me away. Just then, our eighteen-year-old son, David, who had not been on the trip with us, burst in the front door and blurted, "Mom, did you hear about Grandpa? He shot himself and he died." The sheriff had contacted David when I could not be reached.

I was stunned. I could only think that my father had not heard enough about his need to be saved, that I had failed to witness enough. I said over and over, "He wasn't saved; I didn't talk to him as much as I should have." I was beside myself with shock and guilt. I loved my father, and he was now in eternity. I sat on the piano bench, rocking back and forth, holding my arms, and kind of babbling. My five-and-a-half-year-old daughter, Becky, leaned against my knee and whispered, "Be still and know that I am God." As she spoke, the agitation immediately left me. It was as though I had been covered with a cloak of peace, and I was calm.

A little child shall lead them.

Mary Kirk

During the funeral or memorial there are plenty of people around helping and comforting the bereaved. It seems that the worst time for those left behind are not the chaotic first days and weeks but the days, weeks, and months when all the friends and relatives leave and go back to their busy daily lives.

My sister, Linda (whose husband died and left her with two teenage daughters), taught me a lot. As time went on she did what she had to do, but she missed Steve so much. She loved to talk about him, especially the funny and happy times. I, along with many other people, was uncomfortable with this. Linda explained that talking about Steve made her feel close to him. I learned to shut my mouth and just listen; at times I added some of my own funny memories. Linda loved to wear Steve's old T-shirts. It made her feel he was still there with her. For many years she wore his wedding ring on a chain around her neck.

Karen Steinlight

Then they [Job's three friends] sat on the ground with him for seven days and seven nights. No one said a word to him, because they saw how great his suffering was.

Job 2:13

Time

*Little things seem nothing, but they give peace, like
those meadow flowers which individually seem odor-
less but all together perfume the air.*

Georges Bernanos

Charles took one look at my face and laid his hand on
my arm, gently drawing me into a quiet room.

"Tell me."

I can't; I'm so tired of all this weeping. The tears had
swamped me again on the drive to work. Why was I
so vulnerable in the car? Just driving along I'd be fine
and then, like a lightning strike, the tears would burst
forth. Not the quiet kind of tears one sees in a movie,
but the noisy, sight-stealing kind, where you must pull
over to the side of the road or cause an accident.

I thought I'd covered the evidence quite admirably.

But all his years as a counselor, pastor, and AA member had given him a sensitivity to the trauma of tears.

"I am so tired of crying." The words burst forth with more tears.

He handed me his handkerchief. "Anything new?"

I shook my head. "I—I thought I should be over this by now."

His smile told me the lie of my thoughts.

When I'd finally run out of tears again, he sighed with me. "Okay now?"

I nodded. Why was crying alone so different from crying with someone who cared? One kind of weeping felt as if it would never stop, the other like a spring shower that parts to let the sun shine through. We stood, and he hugged me. Two hours from now, he would not remember this brief episode, for his mind no longer retained the short term.

But Charles of the magnificent white hair and the healing touch had been used of God again, to weave one more healing strand in my tapestry of grief.

Mark in your datebook various anniversaries of the griever's loss and let the person know you're thinking of him or her on those dates. Some of the "grief milestones" are: six weeks, three months, six months, one year, two years. Usually by about six weeks after the loss, most of the rest of the world has moved on, and the griever can feel forgotten. Just letting the person know you're remembering the loss can bring more comfort than you know.

Remind the griever that grief is "messy." The emotions are turbulent, unpredictable, and intense. It's okay if they can't make sense of it all. Tell them to try to take one day at a time and know that while time won't make the pain go away, it will make the pain less intense. The length of a time of mourning is not directly proportional to the depth of love felt for the person who has died. Each person's grief time line is unique.

Don't be afraid to mention the person who has died or to relate memories you have of him or her. The grieving person often is greatly relieved to find someone who is willing to reminisce about the person who has died.

Janelle Schneider

Jim and I never married, but he was the most important person in my world, and I was in his. When he committed suicide, I was devastated. My loss was different from any other I've experienced. People did not seem to know what to do—I was not married to Jim, so I was not his next of kin. I received no flowers, few cards, not even valid time off work. But some sweet and brave people did indeed help me.

For the first time in my life, I decided to accept whatever help people offered. I was a teacher, and when my fellow teachers asked what they could do to help, I told them. This event was so traumatic for me that I was literally afraid to be alone, and the long, sleepless nights were pretty awful. So every night, a different coworker showed up at my apartment with a sleeping bag and sacked out on my living room floor so that I would feel safe. Every one of them accepted the fact that I needed to be left alone with my bedroom door closed but assured of their presence on the other side of that door. This went on for a couple of weeks, until I could be alone again. I will never forget what those teachers did for me.

About six weeks after Jim died, I went out of state to visit a friend whom I knew had some understanding of grief. The first night, she gave me C. S. Lewis's *A Grief Observed*, which I read straight through, hooked by the first line: "No one ever told me that grief felt so like fear." That night, for the first time in weeks, I slept more than a couple of hours. In fact, I slept eighteen hours—until my worried friend woke me up. I suddenly became like a person on heavy medication, unable to focus and unable to put any of this together. So my friend gave me one piece of advice, something that helped her when her mother died. She said: "Every time you have a memory about Jim, write it down." Now that may seem really simple, but when the person you loved more than anybody voluntarily abandons you so completely, it's hard to know what to do with that.

I took my friend's advice. In my journal, I would write Jim's name and underline it, followed by any memory of him at all. I wrote pages of conversations I remembered us having. Today I treasure that journal more than any photo album. It helps me recall the beautiful man I loved. In my shock and confusion, I would have lost so much of my sense of him as a three-dimensional being had my friend not made that simple suggestion.

name withheld

We need the star-shine of each other to light our skies and chase the shadows.

Patricia Pinkston in Women's World *magazine*

I pressed "play" on my answering machine.

"Hello, Marlene. This is Carol Stephens. You may not know who I am. This is going to sound crazy; I sat behind you in church on Sunday, and I felt that God was prompting me to call you." The message ended with her apology for calling, but she left her phone number.

I knew who Carol was, but I didn't really know her. We both attended a large church where it was impossible to know everyone. All I knew about her was that she had cancer.

I returned Carol's call and made arrangements to stop by her house to get acquainted. We immediately felt comfortable together. I learned that she had been fighting cancer for quite some time. From what I gathered, her prognosis was not good.

Over the next few months, we chatted by phone, and I dropped by her home for visits.

As Christmas rolled around, we talked about the upcoming holiday. We never verbalized it, but we both knew it would be her last. Carol's energy was severely limited. Together we devised a "plan" to help release some of her expectations, to delegate a few things to family and friends, and to focus on the people she loved—primarily her husband and two teenage sons.

I shopped for some gifts she wanted to give her family and brought her a bright red poinsettia.

The holidays came and went far too quickly. In February, Carol went home to be with her Maker. After a few short months of opening up my heart to this new friend, I now had to release her. Nevertheless, knowing Carol in her last months was indeed a privilege. She modeled a steadfast faith, and I learned not to shrink back from those who are walking through a deep, dark valley.

I also learned the importance of not making assumptions about what others are going through and not minimizing their feelings—just because I am uncomfortable. My natural tendency is to hesitate when someone suffers because I don't know what to say or do. But this experience taught me to get involved, to listen, to ask questions, to be available, and to follow my heart.

Looking back, I find it nothing short of amazing that this quiet-natured, reserved soul picked up the phone and made the call inviting me to share her last months on earth. It was my privilege to call Carol "friend." Perhaps through her, I've learned to serve more graciously those who are hurting.

Marlene Depler

PLEASE DON'T FORGET ME

I once was two
And now I'm one;
No fault of mine
For he's gone home.

You were our friends;
Can you be mine?
For I'm alone—
The extra one.

During the grieving process, most of us live with a difficult something or someone that we do not know how to deal with and do not want to face: a rebellious or hurting child, a house to sell or a move to make, a car to buy, employment advice. In these times, we need someone to lead the way—holding us accountable to the truth about ourselves and our situation and showing us how to dig out. We also need people in our lives to affirm our shattered worth and to applaud our shaky efforts to make a life.

When I needed help the most, God provided a variety of people. They didn't make decisions for me or pay my bills, but they showed me their scars and encouraged me that I, too, would survive. I'm grateful to friends who stacked firewood, helped me shop for a couch, and invited me to dinner. One woman cleaned my kitchen on moving day, others crawled under my house to wire my TV, and one special lady volunteered to be my three-in-the-morning friend.

When friends are there for us, letting us babble and sometimes just cry without feeling that they have to fix our difficulties for us, we can take charge of our lives again. When others have faith in us, we develop faith in ourselves. When they are transparent about their own losses and lead by example, we begin to believe that, in time, we will survive and thrive, too.

Kari West

The death of your child is a loss you never get over—it just becomes part of who you are.

Jodi Gilliland

The memorial service was past and all the gathered family had returned to their real lives, leaving my friend by herself and facing the wrenching reality of life alone.

"Come, Milly, let me take you to lunch." The phone call had taken only a moment.

"Are—are you sure? I'm not very good company."

"Of course I'm sure. I'll pick you up at 12:30. Most of the crowd will be clearing out by then."

Later, sitting in the restaurant, Milly laid the menu aside. "I'm really not very hungry."

"Have the soup. You know they make the best soups here."

"All right."

When the soup and muffins arrived, I took Milly's cold hands in mine and said grace, only to glance up after the amen and see the tears trickling down Milly's cheeks.

"I cry so easy."

"I know. Me too."

We both wiped our tears. With the first spoonful of clam chowder, Milly said, "Henry loved clam chowder."

She didn't stop talking for the next half hour as the waitress took away our bowls, brushed the muffin crumbs off the tablecloth, and refilled the coffee cups.

She talked through a piece of apple pie and another cup of coffee, telling her memories, even laughing at the stories we shared.

"I didn't mean to talk so much; you hardly got to say a word."

"I know." I smiled. "But that's what you needed—and so did I. We'll do this again soon."

And we did.

Elaine Aspelund

Grieving. There is no one way to do it. My sister died after a seven-year battle with cancer. They were hard years, years filled with pain and uncertainty. Yet they were also years of direction, of joy, always being blessed by her sweet, sweet spirit. We enjoyed singing our favorite songs, working on jigsaw puzzles, making spaghetti carbonara for dinner.

One day I sat beside her at a softball game; she was in a wheelchair, clad in sweats with a blanket covering her legs and an umbrella warding off the raindrops. We watched and cheered as her youngest daughter threw the runner out at second. Sure, she would have been more comfortable at home, but there she would have been focused on herself, and she did not want that.

I grieve, yes, but only for a moment; for my sister instilled in me the appreciation for each day. My joy bubbles over and is contagious to others, as I laugh over some trivial thing; that is what my sister would have done. I have hope for bright tomorrows, the willingness to reach out, to touch others, to love God in spite of increasing pain; these are the things I learned at my frail sister's side. This was her legacy, and I cannot mourn her passing, for she would not want it that way. I must go on living life to its fullest. I must seek God's love. I must look for the silver lining. There is one for each of us; it is woven into the fabric of each minute we call life.

No, I do not grieve for her, for she is not here; she has gone on to a better life, and that is where my heart and mind must be.

Birdie Etchison

Some friendships thrive in times of ease and celebration but wane during seasons of grief. We've all had friends who, when put to the test of the various times mentioned in Ecclesiastes chapter three, proved to be fair-weather friends. Ten years ago Shirley Millar gave me the gift of an off-season friendship.

When my dad was diagnosed with cancer and died five months later, Shirley stayed by my side. In a time when others backed away altogether or felt a need to fill the emotional gap with words, usually platitudes, she gave quiet solace. And though she was poised to listen, she wasn't intimidated by the silence when I couldn't speak. She offered the encompassing comfort of a hug and a quiet permission to cry when tears tugged at my eyelids.

Modeling the all-season friendship we have with Jesus, Shirley showed me that a true friend walks through the off-seasons with you as well as through the peak seasons.

Mona Gansberg Hodgson in Silver and Gold: Stories of Special Friendships *(NavPress, 2003)*

Lessons Learned

Happy moments, praise God.
Difficult moments, seek God.
Quiet moments, worship God.
Painful moments, trust God.
Every moment, thank God.

Jane LaMunyon
and Robert McCreery

I have a real down-to-earth friend, Mimi, who stayed by me after my husband died. One day when I was feeling totally overwhelmed she gave me these words of wisdom that have stuck with me through the years: "Phylis, just do Tuesday."

Phylis Moore

I stand at the kitchen counter, phone cradled between shoulder and ear, jotting on a notepad, listening. Listening, as my friend pours out the sad news of the loss of her tiny unborn baby. I wipe away my own tears, understanding all too well the anguish of this mother's broken heart, as I scribble circles and lines—and the words to a song. *"Little one, loved before knowing . . . Precious one, in dreams so fair."*

Only a few weeks before, she'd called, ecstatic about the test confirming the presence on the little life within her. She even rejoiced as nausea began to further confirm the fact. But the nausea abruptly stopped, and the spotting began. And now the baby was gone. . . .

She weeps, and I with her. People don't understand. They smile and pat her shoulder and say she can always have another one. . . . She wants to scream at them, "Don't you see? My unborn baby died! . . . This was a human life—a life I loved. I am grieving!"

I understand. How I understand. *"My empty arms ache to be holding . . ."*

We share. We cry. I tell her I'll bring supper and we hang up. Memories flood back as I sip my tea. . . . Three babies (I wonder what they're like?) wait for me in heaven. . . .

After my third miscarriage, a perfectly beautiful little baby only about an inch long, with fingers and toes and eyes, I cried out to Jesus in my helpless, agonizing loss. And the idea of finding some sort of memorial surfaced. (It's tough, losing a son or daughter so early; there's no funeral, no grave, no memorial. Some people act like there was no baby.) I went shopping, asking the Lord to help me find what He'd chosen. I wandered aisles, not even knowing what I was looking for, and then stopped. A tiny green bush with pink miniature roses sat high on the shelf . . . and I knew I'd found it.

The whole family planted it together that evening in the corner of the yard by the fence. As we patted the soft soil around the little roots, we explained to the children that a rosebud sometimes may begin to swell on this side of the fence, but if the stem grows through that barrier, it actually blooms on the other side. Our baby was like the little rose. He began here, but went on to live with Jesus before he "bloomed"—before we could know him. That seemed to make sense to them. . . .

It wasn't so easy for me. My body had sheltered and nourished a new life and now faced postpartum changes, but with empty arms and a deep, unexplainable longing for my baby whom I already loved. And no one understood. A few women who had personally experienced the loss of an unborn child tried to offer comfort . . . but only the Lord could heal my broken heart.

Many times in the ensuing months I would slip away, alone, down to the corner of the fence to sit by the little rosebush, pluck the weeds and pour out my heart to Father God. . . .

Knowing my babies lived still, just on the other side, I railed against that fence. It represented the painful separation I felt, but it also became the Lord's teaching tool.

It was wire, thin but tall, and I could see through it. The other side was really there, and only a step away—just as heaven is. As He taught me to accept His will . . . He birthed in my heart a new understanding of the reality of heaven and its closeness. Within me the assurance grew that one day in heaven I would hug these precious children who now already live in perfection. And over many months, as I sat beside the little rose in the arms of my Abba Father, my Comforter, my Wonderful Counselor, my Hiding Place, my heart began to heal.

My tea is cold. . . . My eyes drift to the little pink rosebush in the yard. I walk out to pick one for my buttonhole as I make a mental list of dinner preparations for my hurting friend.

Main dish and salad, treats for the children, sympathy card—and a tiny rosebush. There are lovely red ones at the garden center, and I'll take her one tonight with the song on the notepad. . . . I'll promise to pray for her every day in the coming months. And I'll do it, too. Perhaps it will help her along as she begins her healing journey.

I . . . head outside, tearing off the top sheet of the notepad, reading as I walk,

Little one, loved before knowing,
Precious one, in dreams so fair,
My empty arms ache to be holding
My rosebud who blooms over there.
If you had come to be with us
I'd have shown you the stars and the sea;
Now it's *your* eyes that see them eternally clear—
One day you must show them to me.

Yes, Lord, please tell my little ones that one day they must show them to me. . . . And that I love them. Carefully I tuck the song into my pocket, realizing I must get the shopping for dinner underway. And I walk to the car, one foot in heaven.

Jennifer Maze Brown
in Today's Christian Woman,
May/June 1998

One of the most helpful things someone did for me when my husband died was to bring a couple grocery sacks full of paper plates, napkins, cups, garbage bags, and toilet paper to the house. I know the people who did this felt it was "nothing," but it was such a help!

Stephanie Whitson

My mom died on Christmas Eve and we felt it was a special Christmas gift to her to go to heaven at that time. All of her active years she had done so much for all of us. She loved to celebrate Christmas and to give gifts, even though she and Dad lived far below the poverty level. She would give containers of homemade candy to each member of her extended family (thirty-six of us). She always had a gift for the young children and some small thing for each of the rest of us.

In memory of her, I set up a Grandma tree decorated with peppermint canes, chocolate gold-covered coins, and other tasty goodies for all guests who came to our home during the holiday season. It made me feel good to be celebrating in a way she would have loved.

Also, in the summer, I found much comfort tending the types of flowers that she had loved. I gained my love of flowers from her. She had a bushel of prize ribbons for flowers she grew and floral arrangements she had displayed at garden club shows.

I still look for ways to celebrate the lives of my parents and Dick's parents, even if it is only remembering the happy times.

Elsie Larson

It seemed that Sherry died along with her son on that fateful day. She walked around as if in a fog. I called her daily after the memorial service. She never remembered what we had talked about. She would forget that we had made plans to go out to lunch or dinner. I often went to her house and literally dragged her out of bed. I made her get dressed and took her out to eat. She was never hungry, so I would fix food and bring it over for her and her three surviving sons. We talked a lot, and I listened a lot. She, to this day, loves to talk about Justin. Yes, she has her other sons, but she tried to explain to me once how losing one child makes you want to die also. I cannot understand exactly (not having lost a child myself), but I can put my arms around her and hold her as she cries. I tried to always be there for her. She knew she could call me any time just to talk.

Karen Steinlight

The note said, "I went to the toy store and told the clerk, 'My friend's husband just died, and she needs a new bed partner.' Then we squeezed every teddy bear in sight. This is the most huggable one we could find." The note was attached to a beautifully wrapped box that I found on my front porch. Opening it, I lifted out Beary, a vanilla-colored teddy with a gray leather nose. Years later, he continues to sit on my bed by day and serves as a headrest for reading in bed at night. His fake fur body still dries my tears occasionally. Now I watch for teddy bears on sale, so that I can be ready to bless a new widow with a cuddly bear that passes the hug test.

Phylis Moore

When my daughter was fourteen, she had a friend who was dying of leukemia. There was quite a circle of friends who cherished this little girl, and when she died, this circle of friends worked together to create a scrapbook with pictures and mementos. When they were finished, they gave it to the child's mother. It was such a blessing for this woman and for the girls. The girls grieved and healed as they worked on the scrapbook, and the mother and father had this wonderful book of memories told through the eyes of someone else. It seemed like the perfect thing to do for everyone concerned.

Tracie Peterson

Three people stand out in my memory as being especially helpful after my son Justin died: my sister, my now dear friend Karen Steinlight, and my husband, Rob.

My sister flew to Atlanta from Boston after the accident and took over the responsibility for everything. She cared for my two younger boys while Rob, my second son, and I went to Daytona Beach to gather Justin's belongings from his apartment; we held a memorial service on the campus of Embry-Riddle Aeronautical University where he was a student. She planned the memorial service in Atlanta and handled all the responsibilities that needed to be done while providing emotional support to my family.

Karen's daughter, who went to school with my youngest son, was at the house with my sons when we got the news. I had not met Karen, but she stepped in immediately to serve wherever she was needed. I met her for the first time after the memorial service we had for Justin in Atlanta. She took over at the gathering after the service. After that, she would call me to have lunch with her to get me out of the house. Naturally, I would forget, so she would pick me up at my house and take me to hers. I would just sit in my fog and was not very communicative. But Karen kept calling me and taking me to her house for lunch. She was tenacious and wouldn't allow me to sit alone. She has been more than a friend. She has been a lifeline to reality and recovery.

My husband, who was not my boys' father, was also instrumental in my recovery. Our marriage didn't survive, but he remains one of my dearest friends. He was always there just to listen. He never offered platitudes and never gave advice. He simply listened and let me cry. He is still willing to lend a shoulder, seven years later. He's one of my staunchest supporters, and I can get a reality check from him at any time.

Sherry Oberling

When my father died, a friend sent me a beautiful Delft vase filled with dried flowers. Although the flowers disintegrated years ago, I still have the vase as a reminder of my dad and this friend's kindness. I really appreciated the permanence of the gesture.

Lisa Samson

My friend Tina lost her baby in the fourth month of her pregnancy; it was very traumatic for her and her husband, Jeff, as there seemed to be no reason for the baby to have died. Sean and I weren't sure what we could say or do.

In a miscarriage, everyone seems to focus on the mother, which of course they should. But sometimes the father gets left out. So Sean wrote Jeff a note telling him how sorry he was that he had lost his baby. It touched Jeff so much. He said he felt as if no one understood that he was grieving too until Sean wrote him that note.

Rene Gutteridge

At the end of each of my parents' obituaries in the newspaper I asked for good stories or fond memories. My mom died in 1992, and I treasure the responses I received. She touched so many lives for the better. My dad (Scotty) died recently, and I have received some phone calls and cards. The most meaningful one was an inexpensive card from the staff at his retirement home. Everyone loved him and wrote little notes on the card. The note that touched my heart was from a recent Ethiopian immigrant, a poorly educated lady, who cleans the bathrooms; she wrote: I mis Scatny. Aster.

Laurie Nemec

Find "little things" that mean a lot to the griever, indulgences such as chocolates, a new book, pretty writing paper, whatever makes them feel like they are special, then "spoil" them with these little indulgences whenever you can. These remind them that they are valuable in their own right, not just because of their grief.

Janelle Schneider

Offer to drive someone who is grieving on some of the business errands of death such as to the county building to file the will, or to the insurance office, or wherever they need to go.

Cecile Knowles

Lauraine suggested that I write my father a letter to help me in the grieving process. Instead I wrote a letter to myself, believing that if my dad could write to me from heaven this is in part what he would say. This helped me, and perhaps it could help someone else.

Dear Nancy,

Don't cry so. I am happy here. It is so wonderful. I was foolish to be afraid. Wait until you see it, Nancy. You will know that it was not awful that I died to earth. You miss me, I know, but you may also stop missing me so much. You may heal. It is not disloyal. It is not a bad thing. It is a good thing. Nancy, there were things you and I didn't agree on. I want you to take them all to the Lord Jesus and lay them down. I don't want you to feel guilty or feel that there was unfinished business between us. There is not. It is finished. There are also things that you were ashamed of, beliefs that you didn't do enough, weren't enough. Let it all go. I may have contributed to your believing that. I'm sorry. I was wrong. Parents, Nancy, you got to understand, even those who love you and I loved you, still love you, say wrong things, do wrong things. Forgive and leave it all at Jesus' feet. Don't carry any of it anymore.

You are a wonderful daughter, a wonderful woman.

You were at times a trying but wonderful child. I didn't always tell you how wonderful you were though, and how much I liked you. I should have. It was a mistake. My mistake. I'm sorry.

Nanny, I want you to laugh again. I used to worry that you were too serious, and you were sometimes, but I also see now what a cheerful person you can be. I want you to laugh again.

Love,

Dad

Nancy Hird

In June 2002, I lost my sister, at only thirty-four, to breast cancer. I watched her struggle with the disease for a year and a half. I was with her when she died. I have watched her husband and three young children try to go on with life without her. I have watched my mother struggle with her own grief and anger with God. I have seen my own faith grow beyond anything I ever dreamed by going through this experience.

Two years before my sister was diagnosed, my mother was also stricken with breast cancer. She was healed. We thought—"Wow, God got us through that little wrinkle in life. We prayed and he answered our prayers and we survived this trial. Things can only be good from now on, right?" Then the bottom fell out—Patti was diagnosed, she went through surgery and every possible treatment. We prayed and prayed, other people prayed and prayed, and still we lost her.

Books like Lauraine Snelling's *The Healing Quilt* aid in my healing. Her story, written more than fifteen years after her precious daughter died, helps people like me and my mother in our grieving, which is still so fresh in our hearts. Such stories remind us that no matter how devastated we are by whatever life throws at us—God will lift us up and bring us through it.

One thing I have come to realize over the last two years is that I believe there is a plan in life—someday we will know the reasons. That belief has comforted and strengthened me through this trial. I think it will make me better prepared to go through the next one, and I know there will be. Part of that plan must be the way that I just happened to see *The Healing Quilt* on the "new books" shelf at the library and picked it up to read the jacket—God must have led me there, for I had not read any of Snelling's other books.

Jodi Gilliland

Lessons Learned

Someone sent me a book
About a woman who lost
Sons and husband.
She said God carried her through;
She felt grief but no pain.
The hole that is my heart
Shrieks of agony.
My eyes bleed tears.
What is wrong with me?
Where are you, God?

Someone else sent me a book,
Surviving the Loss of a Love.
I read the bits and pieces.
I write in a journal
All my anguish and rage.
Then I hear his voice.
I write what he says
Line after line after line:
I love you. I love you. I love you.
God is indeed here.

These are some of the gifts that meant the most to me after my mother died.

- A ceramic picture frame with pansies on it for a picture of Mom.
- Anything that had pansies, pandas, or cardinals on it, because people knew Mom had a special love for those things and receiving them would remind me of her.
- A beautiful afghan from ChiLibris, a group of writer friends. Something soft and warm to wrap myself in, it reminded me then and still does that people loved me and were thinking of me.
- A gift basket filled with soothing teas, a candle, bath salts, and a CD of soothing music.
- Flowers. Bright, scented flowers.
- Meals. I don't know if that qualifies as a gift, but it was a gift to me that I didn't even have to think about cooking. The church ladies supplied us meals for three months, while Mom was ill and then after she died. I didn't have to cook a single meal. And they didn't bother us with details. They arranged everything, making sure they met our dietary needs and likes. They brought a meal each

day, which gave us a chance for a brief visit. This was an amazing gift.

Most of all, my family and I appreciated notes that shared a memory of my mother.

Karen Ball

Dos and Don'ts for Friends of Grievers

Dos

1. Go to those who are grieving and just be there—hug them, hold them, cry with them.
2. Let them talk.
3. Listen without judging.
4. Sometime soon after the memorial service take them to lunch; two to four months later take them to lunch again.
5. Call and ask if there is anything you can do for them.
6. Tell them you are praying for them and ask for special prayer requests.
7. If a person's spouse has died and they used to come to your place as a couple, keep inviting the griever to join your events.

8. When you are with them, mention their loved one and how much the loved one meant to you too.

Don'ts

1. Don't use platitudes or Scripture verses glibly.
2. Never say that time heals all wounds. It's been thirty-one years since my mother died, and I still miss her terribly. Time doesn't heal—the hurt is probably less acute, but it's still there.
3. Don't forget about them. On Valentine's Day, Christmas Day, and Easter I always send the widows in my church circle a card to let them know they are not forgotten.
4. Don't be judgmental about their feelings. If they feel abandoned by God and say so, just be quiet and listen—don't offer advice.
5. Never say "I know just how you feel." Unless you have lost exactly what they have lost, you haven't a clue of what they are going through.

Elaine Aspelund

More
Helpful Hints

When I was growing up, my grandmother lived with our family. I would curl up on her bed and watch her rock back and forth in her rocking chair, her lap filled with brightly colored yarn and her knitting needles flying. Grandma never missed an opportunity to dispense a little wisdom as she worked. Peering over her glasses she would tell me, "Child, remember this. God never promised us smooth seas. But he did promise us a safe harbor."

Those words didn't mean much to me back then, but I did remember them, and they sure mean a lot to me now. Because I've learned firsthand that life has bad times as well as good, sad times as well as happy, and times of tumultuous storms as well as times of peaceful harbors. I know because I've lived them.

When I was struggling with some of the worst, saddest, most tumultuously stormy times, I came across this prayer written by J. F. Stark in the 1500s, and it blessed me greatly:

Lord! When I am in sorrow, I think on Thee.
Listen to the cry of my heart, and to my sorrowful complaint.
Yet, O Father, I would not prescribe to Thee when and how Thy help should come.

I will willingly tarry for the hour which Thou Thyself hast appointed for my relief.

Meanwhile, strengthen me by Thy Holy Spirit; strengthen my faith, my hope, my trust; give me patience and resolution to bear my trouble; and let me at last behold the time when Thou wilt make me glad with Thy grace.

Ah, my Father! Never yet hast Thou forsaken thy children.

Forsake not me.

Ever doest Thou give gladness unto the sorrowful.

O give it now unto me.

Always doest Thou relieve the wretched.

Relieve me too, when and where and how Thou will.

Unto Thy wisdom, love, and quickness, I leave it utterly.

Amen.

Amen.

Kay Marshall Strom

My husband, Bob, passed away after a long fight with cancer.

Things Bob did that helped me . . .

He planned his funeral in detail. He chose the music and who would perform it, the pallbearers (he asked them personally), and the pastor to give the message (he also asked him personally); he wrote for permission to reprint an A. W. Tozer article, "If I Only Had One Year to Live." The only thing he didn't do was select his own casket and burial plot.

He wrote a several-page booklet titled "To My Children," giving them advice on how to live the Christian life. We found it in his planner after he was gone.

He took me to the attorney and to his office, making sure everything that could possibly be done financially ahead of time was taken care of. Then he asked a friend of ours who is excellent with finances to "take care" of me.

He suggested I make "our room" my office and discussed furniture arrangements of the new office so the transition would be as easy as possible for me.

He never complained and bore the suffering with grace and courage.

He made the decision himself as to when to stop chemotherapy and sign up for hospice; he assured me he felt relief at the decision and that it was the right time and the right thing to do.

He told me my writing career was going to really "take off" after he was gone. While he regretted he wasn't going to be here to see it, he knew it was going to happen, and he was very proud of me.

He initiated the selection of a newer car for me so I would have reliable transportation after he was gone.

He told me how precious I was to him and what a blessing I was in his life.

He said, "Wherever cancer takes us is a place to share our faith," and he modeled it. Now I say, "Wherever widowhood takes me is a place to share my faith," and I'm trying to live up to that.

He organized all his original music, recorded it, and had copies made for each member of the family.

He tried to save his best energy for his family by limiting visitors and the time they could spend with him.

He encouraged his kids to continue their normal lives. (The night before he died was Winter Banquet at the Christian school, and he insisted that Zachary and Shannon take their dates and go.)

As to what people did for me that was meaningful, what really sticks out is one woman at church who never said anything but always gave me a hug and a pat on the shoulder when she saw me in the hall alone.

Also, the day Bob died, our dearest friends immediately came to the house and stayed with us. They brought in food, they sat and talked, and they laughed, sharing good memories of Bob. It was so comforting to hear laughter in my house that day.

Two men helped me by taking the bed out of the house. For me it was very important that I not have to face the bed. They took it down and rearranged the furniture in the bedroom so there wasn't a big gap in the room. I hadn't been sleeping in the bed anyway, so I didn't need it, and I didn't want to have to face it.

Stephanie Whitson

Something I learned as I staggered through the holidays after Marie died: No matter what day it is, it is still only twenty-four hours long.

I found this quote by Dylan Thomas to be very comforting and very true: "After the first death, there is no other." Once you have truly experienced the death of someone or something you love, you know you will survive the grief that accompanies it. For me, it was the death of a beloved cat. I had had a grandfather die and several other people, but that cat was the "first death."

In *The Once Again Prince* Irving Townsend wrote, "We who choose to surround ourselves with lives more temporary than our own, live within a fragile circle easily and often breached. Unable to accept its awful gaps, we still would live no other way. We cherish memory as the only certain immortality, never fully understanding the necessary plan."

This was written on the occasion of the death of a horse. It's fitting for any animal companion, however.

Woodeene Koenig Bricker

One of the hardest things for me was to watch my husband's life shrink back until his world was incredibly small. His greatest delights were to cuddle his stuffed horse, to have all the potato chips he could eat, to be able to sleep whenever he wanted, and to have me beside him reading out loud.

I would look down at my shrunken husband and plead through my tears, "Oh, God, please . . . please . . ." and then I would stop, because I didn't know what else to say.

It is so difficult to deal with raw, stark reality and not lose hope. It's so hard to continue to pray in faith and at the same time remain open to answers you don't want to accept.

Helplessness overwhelmed me, and God seemed very far away.

And yet it is precisely at such times, when we feel least like praying, that we most need to pour our hearts out to our Lord. In the midst of our toughest times, in the most challenging of situations, that's when we have the greatest opportunities to learn how great and complete and perfect God's love really is.

My grandmother, who loved nothing more than to get outside on a sunny day and work in her garden, used to have a pillow embroidered with these words:

"Sunshine all the time makes a desert." It's true! We were never meant to live our lives in nothing but sunshiny happiness and comfort. If we did, how would we get to know the faithfulness of our God? How could we ever experience the joy that comes from trusting him?

How should you pray when your pain and anguish are too deep for words? Ask God to help you accept his loving wisdom. If you can manage it, thank him that he is in control. If you cannot, ask him to bring you to the place where you can. Pray for faith. Pray for perseverance and endurance. And pray that now, when you need him so much, God will hold you close to his loving heart.

Kay Marshall Strom

DADDY'S GIRLS

We stood together—the four
daughters of Bill,
watching grave dirt
mingle with memories,
listening to the robin
sing from the branches
of a towering juniper,
and praying for lessons.

Mona Gansberg Hodgson

Another type of grief that I have gone through is losing a beloved pet. I have worked at different veterinarian offices and have seen people go through very deep grief over the death of their animal. In fact, grief counseling for these people is offered through the animal hospital where I used to work. I think this type of loss is hardest on people who never had children; they think of their animals as their kids. I still miss my Rottweiler so very much. He was my best friend. He never told me I was overweight, had pimples or bad breath. He just loved me as I was. Wow, if only we humans could love like that. The best help in relieving some of the pain of missing him was having my daughter bring her German shepherd with her when she moved back to live with us. He is a sweet dog that helps fill up the hole that Grizzly left.

Karen Steinlight

An odd by-product of my loss is that I'm aware of being an embarrassment to everyone I meet. At work, at the club, in the street, I see people, as they approach me, trying to make up their minds whether they'll "say something about it" or not. I hate it if they do, and if they don't. Some funk it altogether. R. has been avoiding me for a week. I like best the well-brought-up young men, almost boys, who walk up to me as if I were a dentist, turn very red, get it over, and then edge away to the bar as quickly as they decently can. Perhaps the bereaved ought to be isolated in special settlements like lepers.

C. S. Lewis in A Grief Observed

BOXING GOD

Striving to fashion
darkness into soothing lines,
I cry, "If only. . . ."
I tug on cardboard
flaps, reaching for more packing
tape, I argue, "Why?"
Pressed by life, I fold.
That's when God envelops me
whispering, "I AM."

Mona Gansberg Hodgson

A sick man turned to his doctor as he was leaving the room after paying a visit and said, "Doctor, I am afraid to die. Tell me what lies on the other side."

Very quietly the doctor said, "I don't know."

"You don't know? You, a Christian man, do not know what is on the other side?"

The doctor was holding the handle of the door. On the other side of the door there came the sound of scratching and whining. As he opened the door a dog sprang into the room and leaped on him with an eager show of gladness.

Turning to the patient, the doctor said, "Did you notice that dog? He had never been in this room before. He did not know what was inside. He knew nothing except that his master was here, and when the door opened he sprang in without fear. I know little of what is on the other side of death, but I do know one thing: I know my Master is there, and that is enough. And when the door opens, I shall pass through with no fear, but with gladness."

author unknown

Looking back, the greatest gifts were people
Who comforted with:
A touch of love,
A listening ear,
A shoulder that absorbed tears,
A healing hug,
A portion of their precious time.

All of that
Is God—
With skin on.

Suggested Reading

Colgrove, Melba, Harold H. Bloomfield, and Peter McWilliams. *How to Survive the Loss of a Love*. Los Angeles: Prelude, 1991.

Ehman, Karen, Kelly Hovermale, and Trish Smith. *Homespun Gifts from the Heart*. Grand Rapids: Revell, 2003.

Elliot, Elisabeth. *The Path of Loneliness: Finding Your Way through the Wilderness to God*. Grand Rapids: Revell, 2004. First published 1988 by Nelson.

Lewis, C. S. *A Grief Observed*. San Francisco: HarperCollins, 1994. First published 1961 by Faber (London).

Moore, Phylis. *He Gathers Your Tears: Words of Comfort for a Widow's Heart.* Grand Rapids: Revell, 2002.

Sittser, Gerald L. *A Grace Disguised: How the Soul Grows through Loss.* Grand Rapids: Zondervan, 1996.

Smith, Harold Ivan. *A Decembered Grief: Living with Loss while Others Are Celebrating.* Boston: Beacon Hill, 1999.

Zonnebelt-Smeenge, Susan J., and Robert C. De Vries. *Getting to the Other Side of Grief: Overcoming the Loss of a Spouse.* Grand Rapids: Baker, 1998.

Lauraine Snelling is an award-winning author of over fifty books, both fiction and nonfiction, for adults and young adults. She has two horse series for young teen girls, the Golden Filly series and High Hurdles series. Lauraine is also the author of the popular Red River of the North series set in North Dakota in the last part of the nineteenth century. The Bjorklund brothers bring their families from Norway to begin a new life on the land they will turn from prairie to fertile farms. Dakotah Treasures is the most recent series.

Turning to contemporary novels, *The Healing Quilt* is the story of four women, mending their broken hearts one stitch at a time. It comforts women of all ages, as will *The Way of Women.*

Besides writing books and articles, Lauraine teaches at writer's conferences across the country and has an active speaking career. She and her husband, Wayne, have two grown sons, four granddogs, and live in the country where Lauraine can garden, sew, do crafts, cross stitch, enjoy her birds, and eventually have a horse again.